The Lantern out of Doors

An Experiment in Emulating the Early Church Gatherings

Eugene Luning

Copyright © 2016 Eugene Luning

All rights reserved.

Scriptural quotations used in this work are taken from the Holy
Bible, New International Version®, NIV®. Copyright © 1973,
1978, 1984, 2011 by Biblica, Inc.™ All rights reserved
worldwide.

ISBN: 1535127481
ISBN-13: 978-1535127486

To those friends and firebrands who
always push us to desire more of Jesus

Foreword

I	Complete Belief in the Power of Prayer	9
II	Together in the Teachings of Jesus	13
III	Complete Belief that Jesus and the Holy Spirit would Act, Speak & Lead by Direct Revelation	19
IV	Attractive & Accepting, Exhibiting a "Kindness that Leads to Repentance"	25
V	Practical	29
VI	Indivisible & Focused on Unity Open to All the Gifts	36
VII	Led by Shepherds who Bore the Stamp of Jesus	51
VIII	Encouraged by, and Encouraging with, the Spirit of Jesus	56
IX	They Gathered Together Constantly	62
X	Devoid of Self & Desirous to Serve	65
XI	Partakers Together of the Bread & the Wine	71
XII	Worshippers	74
	All Conclusions Compiled	76
	Preparations & Questions to be Answered	81
	Recommended Format	83

THE LANTERN OUT OF DOORS

Sometimes a lantern moves along the night,
That interests our eyes. And who goes there?
I think; where from and bound, I wonder, where,
With, all down darkness wide, his wading light?

Men go by me whom either beauty bright
In mould or mind or what not else makes rare:
They rain against our much-thick and marsh air
Rich beams, till death or distance buys them quite.

Death or distance soon consumes them: wind
What most I may eye after, be in at the end
I cannot, and out of sight is out of mind.

Christ minds: Christ's interest, what to avow or amend
There, éyes them, heart wánts, care haúnts, foot fóllows kínd,
Their ránsom, théir rescue, ánd first, fást, last friénd.

Gerard Manley Hopkins

"The fresh air of Heaven blows gustily through these pages
[of the Book of Acts], and the sense that ordinary human life
is continually open to the Spirit of God is very marked. There
is not yet a dead hand of tradition; there is not over-
organization to stifle initiative; there is neither security nor
complacency to destroy sensitivity to the living God. The
early Church lived dangerously, but never before has such a
handful of people exerted such widespread influence. There is
a courage to match the vision; there is a flexible willingness to
match the divine leadership. And there is that unshakable
certainty against which persecution, imprisonment, and death
prove quite powerless."

J.B. Phillips

Summer 2016

This short work is a treatise on treating the Early Church's gatherings as more than some long-forgotten dream, patterns that slipped from our grasp millennia ago, power that we've never known or experienced. Instead, together, we'll consider what we *can* know from the evidence of the New Testament – both in Acts and the Epistles – and we'll invite the Holy Spirit to illuminate our understanding and our attempts to emulate them. We won't be going after *general* admonitions directed toward the Early Church by Paul and the others; we want the *specifics* of what it looked like, felt like, tasted like, sounded like and, overall, just how robust was their shared experience of the Living Jesus.

To consider such spirit and structure, we have to begin with the best-known description of their lifestyle which, it just so happens, is given right at the beginning, in Acts 2:

> *"[The believers] devoted themselves to the apostles' teaching and to fellowship, to the breaking of bread and to prayer. Everyone was filled with awe at the many wonders and signs performed by the apostles. All the believers were together and had everything in common. They sold property and possessions to give to anyone who had need. Every day they continued to meet together in the temple courts. They broke bread in their homes and ate together with glad and sincere hearts, praising God and enjoying the favor of all the people. And the Lord added to their number daily those who were being saved."*

As we read those words, we're equally apt to be delighted or discouraged, thinking either "Let's do that again!" or "Where along the way did we lose that?" Yet it's that second line of thinking – the sense that somehow Jesus has changed in His ways or plan or power toward us – that I'd ask you to be rid of, *right this minute.* You see, the main purpose of this work is to harness our sense of wonder of what's possible in His Body to the illimitable resources that are available in the Holy Spirit – that very One who animated the every day of Jesus' life, the One who was the lifeblood of the first generation of our Brothers and Sisters.

In essence, you and I must begin by *believing*.

I began my studies by scouring the pages of the New Testament for every reference specific to the physical gathering-together of the Early Church believers. Again, not *general* sorts of teachings; words about their gatherings, their meetings, their fellowship. According to my count, there were 77 such references.

Then, with prayer, I printed and scattered these scriptures across my kitchen countertop, read them over and over again, and asked the Lord to sort them into clearer "categories" for our consideration. After an afternoon, I began to see twelve such sub-sections. From there, I considered the historical timing of each of those twelve separate categories and then placed them into a chronological – not necessarily consequential – ordering. Those will be the chapters that comprise this short work, described by their chapter-titles.

At the end of each chapter, after attempting to bring the italicized scriptures into a clearer focus and understanding, I'll offer my own conclusion about what that chapter means for us. After that, you'll see it written: YOUR CONCLUSIONS. Here, I'd be delighted if you'd write in any thoughts or questions or scriptures or ponderings of your own, in order to continue to hone the idea of our eventual gathering. I truly want this to be a shared experience together.

May these pages encourage your heart and enliven your desire that Jesus Himself would enter this world – *and our lives* – in ever greater measure. I'm grateful that you would join me on this journey!

- Eugene

I.

COMPLETE BELIEF IN THE POWER OF PRAYER

The very first recorded activity of any Early Church gathering was prayer. In the moments directly after Jesus' Ascension, we read this:

> *"Then the apostles returned to Jerusalem from the hill called the Mount of Olives, a Sabbath day's walk from the city. When they arrived, they went upstairs to the room where they were staying. Those present were Peter, John, James and Andrew; Philip and Thomas, Bartholomew and Matthew; James son of Alphaeus and Simon the Zealot, and Judas son of James. They all joined together constantly in prayer, along with the women and Mary the mother of Jesus, and with his brothers." (Acts 1)*

Imagine if you yourself had been there. Imagine only having just watched as your Friend, your Savior, your Master, your Teacher, your Risen Lord suddenly flew up into the clouds in a blast of blinding light. Two angels then told you that it was time to stop staring up. Dazed, you walked back into the city, whispering hushed conversations.

Then, as a group, you came together in the very same room where Jesus had once washed your feet, shared a meal with you, spoken of the coming Holy Spirit, and you did what? Prayed. "They all joined together *constantly* in prayer."

But, my friends, have you ever stopped to consider that when the first believers bowed their heads, lifted up their hands, opened their lips to speak to the Almighty One, that they were the first people in history to pray to – and in the Name of – their best and dearest friend? Imagine being a John or James or Peter or Mary Magdalene, with the smell of Jesus' garments still clinging to your nostrils, and then beginning to pray, "Jesus, it's me…"

Our gatherings must always begin with prayer – *that* sort of prayer. We must be characterized by a firsthand, natural, face-to-face style of prayer that allows for no sense of externalized distance between the pray-er and the fully-present Hearer. For there *is* no distance between us anymore! Jesus' shed blood ensures our confident approach and complete proximity to the ear of the One upon the throne – forevermore.

To the Early Church, gathering in prayer was a manifestation of power. When trouble confronted them, they were fearless because they knew that prayer aligned their lives with the ever-available might of the King of Heaven, as evidenced in Acts 12:

> *"So Peter was kept in prison, but the church was earnestly praying to God for him."*

These prayers weren't offered out of fear, but with a certainty that their prayers were directly accomplishing something – an actual hearing before Jesus, the Righteous Judge.

Conversely, when their circumstances were "better," we see the Early Church's posture in prayer shifting, not to laxity, but to an increased hunger for better alignment and for further expressions of His power upon the earth. Consider how the gathering prayed after Peter and John's release from trial before the Sanhedrin, in Acts 4 –

> *On their release, Peter and John went back to their own people and reported all that the chief priests and the elders had said to them. When they heard this, they raised their voices together in prayer to God. "Sovereign Lord," they said, "you made the heavens and the earth and the sea, and everything in them. You spoke by the Holy Spirit through the mouth of your servant,*

THE LANTERN OUT OF DOORS

our father David: 'Why do the nations rage and the peoples plot in vain? The kings of the earth rise up and the rulers band together against the Lord and against his anointed one.'

"Indeed Herod and Pontius Pilate met together with the Gentiles and the people of Israel in this city to conspire against your holy servant Jesus, whom you anointed. They did what your power and will had decided beforehand should happen. Now, Lord, consider their threats and enable your servants to speak your word with great boldness. Stretch out your hand to heal and perform signs and wonders through the name of your holy servant Jesus."

Rather than praying against possible future persecutions, trials or imprisonments, the gathering instead gave praise and then asked for greater boldness and more outpouring of signs and wonders in the name of Jesus. At no point, here, do their prayers bemoan their circumstances. Their circumstances were seen as the stage upon which the power of Jesus might be manifest.

Additionally, praying in the reality of "one Body and one Spirit," the apostles viewed their prayers as both unifying and bonding, despite any physical distance or present separation. Listen to Paul:

"I urge you, brothers and sisters, by our Lord Jesus Christ and by the love of the Spirit, to join me in my struggle by praying to God for me." (Romans 15)

Paul is urging the gathering to pray for him as a way to join him – both volitionally and spiritually – in the calling he'd been given by Jesus. He clearly drew comfort and courage from knowing such prayer was ongoing on his behalf.

Lastly, when looking at the gathering's structure for engaging in corporate prayer, we are given the following instruction by Paul in 1 Timothy 2:

> *"I urge, then, first of all, that petitions, prayers, intercession and thanksgiving be made for all people — for kings and all those in authority, that we may live peaceful and quiet lives in all godliness and holiness. This is good, and pleases God our Savior, who wants all people to be saved and to come to a knowledge of the truth."*

We get the picture of the people joining together in open-ended "petitions, prayers, intercession and thanksgiving" for "all people," with the only specificity being that "kings and all those in authority" be included. These prayers were meant to take into account the purpose and desire of the Lord's heart: that all people have the chance of salvation and to know the truth of Jesus.

CONCLUSION: The *spirit* of the gathering's prayer-life matters more than its *structure*. In the Early Church, they prayed constantly, intimately, fearlessly, emboldeningly, in unity, and – together – "for all people."

It would seem best that we should start our times together in open-ended, unguided prayer that is a reflection of our individual, and yet corporate, face-to-face intimacy with Jesus. Really, prayer should be the greatest characterization of our gathering.

YOUR CONCLUSIONS:

II.

TOGETHER IN THE TEACHINGS OF JESUS

When Jesus spoke, His words were as natural to His hearers as a spring breeze, a summer rainshower, a lofty birdsong, the sounds of the sea. Yet they were also powerful like an unexpected thunderclap on a sunny day, a storm-tossed ocean, an earthquake that shifts everyone and everything upon its surface. Jesus' teachings were His first-hand accounts of the Kingdom of Heaven. They weren't intended to show how different is the Kingdom of Heaven when compared to the ways of the world; they were intended to show that there actually is no way *but* the Kingdom.

Perhaps the greatest measure of the power of Jesus' style of teaching is the fact that it took more than thirty years for the first Gospel – THE GOSPEL OF MARK – to be written down for future generations. Before its appearance, the Early Church passed along the teachings and events of Jesus' life simply by relating them, person to person, heart to heart.

Can you imagine sitting in a room with Peter or James or John and seeing them smile, then suddenly laugh, because a memory of Jesus happened to come to mind? "Oh, you should've *been* there!" they'd say, and then launch into the Feeding of the 5,000, or the Sermon on the Mount, or the Calming of the Storm, or the Healing of Bartimaeus…

Our gatherings must center around the teachings of Jesus alone – in His own natural, powerful style – and on speaking of Him as delightedly, personally, curiously, and directly as we see the Early Church teachers speaking. Second-hand teaching will have no place in our midst. We will speak only of that which He Himself spoke, taught, lived and personified, and only in the manner in which He

Himself spoke it, taught it, lived it, and brought it to life. We're after direct revelation from His Word and by His Holy Spirit. A teacher in our gathering must speak with the joy and spirit of Jesus alone.

In fact, consider just how serious were the Early Church gatherings about keeping Jesus' teaching as the *only* vein of teaching in their midst:

> *"Anyone who runs ahead and does not continue in the teaching of Christ does not have God; whoever continues in the teaching has both the Father and the Son. If anyone comes to you and does not bring this teaching, do not take them into your house or welcome them." (2 John)*

So how will you and I, today, "continue in the teaching" of a One who lived 2,000 years ago; a Man that none of us has ever personally met in the flesh? Firstly, we must begin by seeing our lives as a direct extension of the historical movement of the Gospel; just as much a part of the Kingdom-work as the first Apostles once were. Let's return again to the beginnings, this time in Acts 1:

> *"In those days Peter stood up among the believers (a group numbering about a hundred and twenty) and said, 'Brothers and sisters, the Scripture had to be fulfilled in which the Holy Spirit spoke long ago through David concerning Judas, who served as guide for those who arrested Jesus. He was one of our number and shared in our ministry… For," said Peter, "it is written in the Book of Psalms: 'May his place be deserted; let there be no one to dwell in it,' and, 'May another take his place of leadership.' Therefore it is necessary to choose one of the men who have been with us the whole time the Lord Jesus was living among us, beginning from John's baptism to the time when Jesus was taken up from us. For one of these must become a witness with us of his resurrection."*

It's clear that Peter no longer views himself as just some

simple fisherman from the Galilee; he has begun to place his life within the context of the generational arc of the scriptures, promises and prophecies. We must each do likewise, every single day of our lives. Most people in the Modern Church are comfortable enough describing themselves as "chosen by God," but very few seem to live from the reality that we've been chosen by Jesus *for something*. And it's only our knowledge of Jesus Himself that will create that infinite difference.

In 1 John 1, in one of his most emphatic stretches of writing, the Apostle John, the "disciple whom Jesus loved," lays the groundwork for how we're all meant to approach Jesus:

> *"We are writing to you about something which has always existed yet which we ourselves actually saw and heard: something which we had an opportunity to observe closely and even to hold in our hands, and yet, as we know now, was something of the very Word of life himself! For it was life which appeared before us: we saw it, we are eye-witnesses of it, and are now writing to you about it. It was the very life of all ages, the life that has always existed with the Father, which actually became visible in person to us mortal men. We repeat, we really saw and heard what we are now writing to you about. We want you to be with us in this — in this fellowship with the Father, and Jesus Christ his Son."*

The bedrock for teaching of Jesus must ever and always be our intimacy with, connection to, abiding in, and drawing our life from Jesus – "life himself." The Apostles' realization that their friend was actually **LIFE** completely transformed the way they lived and the way they taught within the Early Church gatherings. In fact, the Apostle Paul famously resolved to know *only* Jesus and the power of His life and death, as he wrote in 1 Corinthians 2:

> *"For I resolved to know nothing while I was with you except*

Jesus Christ and him crucified. I came to you in weakness with great fear and trembling. My message and my preaching were not with wise and persuasive words, but with a demonstration of the Spirit's power, so that your faith might not rest on human wisdom, but on God's power. We do, however, speak a message of wisdom among the mature, but not the wisdom of this age or of the rulers of this age, who are coming to nothing. No, we declare God's wisdom, a mystery that has been hidden and that God destined for our glory before time began."

If we're prepared to focus *only* on Jesus in our teaching, we become fit vessels for "a demonstration of the Spirit's power" and the revelation of "a mystery that has been hidden and that God destined for our glory." For us, everything else should be as dross.

And yet there might be some who'd argue that if we center solely on Jesus in our teaching, we'll lose the Kingdom's directed directives for ministering to the world around us. Not so. Instead, consider the way we're actually *sent* by our complete concentration on the person of Jesus, and by our gathering's living its whole life "in Christ" -

"Therefore, if anyone is in Christ, the new creation has come: The old has gone, the new is here! All this is from God, who reconciled us to himself through Christ and gave us the ministry of reconciliation: that God was reconciling the world to himself in Christ, not counting people's sins against them. And he has committed to us the message of reconciliation. We are therefore Christ's ambassadors, as though God were making his appeal through us. We implore you on Christ's behalf: Be reconciled to God. God made him who had no sin to be sin for us, so that in him we might become the righteousness of God." (2 Cor. 5)

Our constant focus on Jesus – and on the mysteries, power and inheritance gained by our life "in" Him – lead directly to our taking on His personal ministry – "the ministry of reconciliation." In essence, we become more ready to be impelled by the One who now indwells us. And it's only when our eyes are trained upon *Him* that we ever learn to operate as "Christ's ambassadors"; it's only by abiding in *Him* that He can "make his appeal *through* us." Our gathering's teaching must teach such self-abandonment that only *He* lives.

And, finally, we must never stop talking about, teaching on, discussing and delighting in the access that is ours – this is one of the highest outcomes for which Jesus chose to shed His blood:

> *"Therefore, brothers and sisters, since we have confidence to enter the Most Holy Place by the blood of Jesus, by a new and living way opened for us through the curtain, that is, his body, and since we have a great priest over the house of God, let us draw near to God with a sincere heart and with the full assurance that faith brings, having our hearts sprinkled to cleanse us from a guilty conscience and having our bodies washed with pure water. Let us hold unswervingly to the hope we profess, for he who promised is faithful. And let us consider how we may spur one another on toward love and good deeds, not giving up meeting together, as some are in the habit of doing, but encouraging one another — and all the more as you see the Day approaching." (Hebrews 10)*

According to the writer of Hebrews, the **purpose** of "meeting together" was to "encourage one another" and "spur one another on toward love and good deeds," **because**, as "brothers and sisters," we now "have confidence to enter the Most Holy Place by the blood of Jesus" and may now "draw near to God with a sincere heart and with...full assurance." Our gathering together – and our "continuing in the teachings of Christ" together – are meant to have us standing in the Throneroom of Heaven together. Nothing less and nothing more.

CONCLUSION: The target of our teaching must be

Jesus Himself – His incarnation, life, teachings, miracles, death, resurrection, ascension, and the inheritance He's given us. Our teachers must always approach *Him* before approaching the gathering. Their teaching must exhibit a flavor of that first-hand, original, "oral tradition" style that we see utilized by the original Disciples and Apostles. And that style can only be learned in the presence of Jesus Himself, by having personal experiences of His voice, His power, His present "aliveness."

Lastly, it would seem that teaching was neither less nor more important than any other element of the Early Church gatherings; that it was integral, but not the lofty thing we often make it. It was simply *part* of what happened whenever they came together. And so it must be for us, as well.

YOUR CONCLUSIONS:

III.

COMPLETE BELIEF THAT JESUS AND THE HOLY SPIRIT WOULD ACT, SPEAK AND LEAD BY DIRECT REVELATION

Our sense that Jesus' personal ministry ended on the hilltop where He ascended is perhaps the most incorrect thinking that exists in the Modern Church. There was not an ounce of that thought within the Early Church gatherings. Those men and women lived their everyday with the continuous thought that Jesus' life was contiguously happening within, and around, their own daily lives. When decisions needed to be made, *He* would be the One to make them. When strategy needed to be set, *He* would be the One to set it. When they confronted sickness, sin, the lost, kings and governors, struggles within the Body, *He* was their first and only recourse.

Consider, for instance, the first "personnel decision" the Early Church ever made, in Acts 1:

> *[Peter said:] "Therefore it is necessary to choose one of the men [to replace Judas Iscariot] who have been with us the whole time the Lord Jesus was living among us, beginning from John's baptism to the time when Jesus was taken up from us. For one of these must become a witness with us of his resurrection.' So they nominated two men: Joseph called Barsabbas (also known as Justus) and Matthias. Then they prayed, 'Lord, you know everyone's heart. Show us which of these two you have chosen to take over this apostolic ministry, which Judas left to go where he belongs.' Then they cast lots, and the lot fell to Matthias; so he was added to the eleven apostles."*

These brothers and sisters believed that Jesus was not only *present* to their present circumstances, aware of what they were up to, but also that He was eminently able to cast the deciding vote for them. When they were praying "Show us which of these two you have chosen," it wasn't in some vague "knowing God's will" way; no, *they actually wanted* **Him** *to decide.*

We must come to trust in His Presence in that same way. We must approach our every decision with a firmness that His voice is final. Truly, we'd be far better off casting lots *in His Presence* than in forming endless exploratory committees and closed-door councils *apart from Him.*

Along those same lines, let's also look at how the first missionary journey in the Church's history coalesced; what were the steps that foreran its sending-out:

> *"Now in the church at Antioch there were prophets and teachers: Barnabas, Simeon called Niger, Lucius of Cyrene, Manaen (who had been brought up with Herod the tetrarch) and Saul. While they were worshiping the Lord and fasting, the Holy Spirit said, 'Set apart for me Barnabas and Saul for the work to which I have called them.' So after they had fasted and prayed, they placed their hands on them and sent them off." (Acts 13)*

As far as we can see, these prophets and teachers had no visible "vision" for "missions"; they were simply together, enjoying Jesus, worshipping and fasting, with their ears wide open. And then the Holy Spirit actually spoke to them. And they actually listened. They didn't ask themselves, "Was that Him?" and then belabor the point with endless backs-and-forths about the nature of "call" and "missions" and "hearing His voice." They simply "fasted and prayed, they placed their hands on them and sent them off." Oh, that we would learn to listen and act so nimbly, so quickly!

So off went Saul and Barnabas on that very first journey, the first foray of the Gospel into "ends of the earth" territory. Daily, they followed only the direct leadings of the Living Jesus…

And yet then how, we might ask, can the members who are "out there," physically separated from the sending-gathering, know how to stay aligned with the rest of what the Body's doing? The Holy Spirit will intervene *again*, Paul later explains:

> *"I went [to Jerusalem] in response to a revelation and, meeting privately with those esteemed as leaders, I presented to them the gospel that I preach among the Gentiles. I wanted to be sure I was not running and had not been running my race in vain."* (Galatians 2)

Paul chose to interrupt his fruitful ministry of teaching and preaching, traveling all over the Mediterranean world, because he'd received a "revelation" from Jesus – a vision. The Apostle Paul, one of the most intellectually gifted thinkers in the history of the Church, was personally able to be led by a supernatural vision from His Lord. Yet, again, consider the roots from which the Early Church's belief had grown:

> *"'Now, Lord, consider [the Sanhedrin's] threats and enable your servants to speak your word with great boldness. Stretch out your hand to heal and perform signs and wonders through the name of your holy servant Jesus.' After they prayed, the place where they were meeting was shaken. And they were all filled with the Holy Spirit and spoke the word of God boldly."* (Acts 4)

When that prayer was being prayed, Paul (then Saul) was still a Pharisee and he hadn't even begun to sharpen his knives for the flesh of the Way-followers. And yet, just a few years later, he *himself* was consumed by those "signs and wonders"; *he* was shaken forever by the earthquake of the Holy Spirit's ability to manifest.

And speaking of manifestations within the Early Church gatherings...

> *"Is anyone among you sick? Let them call the elders of the church to pray over them and anoint them with oil in the name of the Lord. And the prayer offered in faith will make the sick person well; the Lord will raise them up. If they have sinned, they will be forgiven. Therefore confess your sins to each other and pray for each other so that you may be healed. The prayer of a righteous person is powerful and effective." (James 5)*

When the members of the Early Church confronted physical ailments, they approached them in the spirit of James' words and by the direct power of Jesus. In essence, sickness called for healing; Jesus was able to heal; Jesus now lived in them; thus, they would anoint with oil, pray and, likewise, heal. Throughout the Book of Acts, there never seemed to be much second-guessing about praying for direct healing; they trusted that such prayers were *always* "in His will." They'd personally watched the way that Jesus would walk into a town, proclaim the Kingdom, and then, by its power, heal "great numbers of people who were suffering from various forms of disease" (Mark 1). Remember, they didn't believe that His personal ministry had ended at the Ascension – if they saw Him doing it, they believed they should be doing it too.

Finally, how did the Early Church gatherings assess "success" in their ministry strategies; what was the proof that something they did was, in Heaven's economy, "working?" Consider Peter's example in Acts 10:

> *"While Peter was still speaking these words [in Cornelius' house], the Holy Spirit came on all who heard the message. The circumcised believers who had come with Peter were astonished that the gift of the Holy Spirit had been poured out even on Gentiles. For they heard them speaking in tongues and praising God. Then Peter said, 'Surely no one can stand in the way of their being baptized with water. They have received the Holy Spirit just as we have.' So he ordered that they be baptized in the name of Jesus Christ."*

Short and sweet: If the powerful, palpable presence of the Holy Spirit is present, whatever the gathering is presently doing is working. But if it's lots of human effort, fleshly frustration, high-input-for-low-output, we've begun to do things on our own again. Just look at how quickly the original Disciples were willing to accept the Gentiles into the Body, given the evidence of that Holy Spirit's presence alone:

> *[Peter:] "'As I began to speak, the Holy Spirit came on them as he had come on us at the beginning. Then I remembered what the Lord had said: 'John baptized with water, but you will be baptized with the Holy Spirit.' So if God gave them the same gift he gave us who believed in the Lord Jesus Christ, who was I to think that I could stand in God's way?' When [the gathering in Jerusalem] heard this, they had no further objections and praised God, saying, 'So then, even to Gentiles God has granted repentance that leads to life.'" (Acts 11)*

We must not relegate the role of the Holy Spirit to some dark mysterious spiritual corner, "only for certain denominations," a force mostly unknown to most Christians. We so often trivialize this One that Jesus called the "power from on high" (Luke 24), the very power that was the lifeblood of the Early Church gatherings. Indeed, we're told by Jesus that "if you then, though you are evil, know how to give good gifts to your children, how much more will your Father in Heaven **give** the Holy Spirit to those who ask him!" (Luke 11) We're actually *meant* to be asking for – and receiving more – of this Holy Spirit! And just look at how imperative His presence was for the first believers:

> *"When the apostles in Jerusalem heard that Samaria had accepted the word of God, they sent Peter and John to Samaria. When they arrived, they prayed for the new believers there that they might receive the Holy Spirit..." (Acts 8)*

The first Apostles wouldn't allow for anyone *not* to receive the wondrous gift of the Holy Spirit's presence and power in their lives. To them, it would've been an unconscionable thought to live a single day without the *full* experience of the glory of the Indwelling.

CONCLUSION: Our gathering should expect to see nothing less than everything we see Jesus and the Holy Spirit doing across the pages of the New Testament. But seeing is not believing. *Believing* is seeing. When it comes to our own decision-making and direct strategic initiatives, we must wait for, watch for, and be expectant of the evidence of His voice and action. We must be open to supernatural visions, physical manifestations, "signs and wonders"; we must be ready to heal and to see His Holy Spirit act through us.

And, again, it's the degree to which we'll *believe* wherein we'll see His ability to act, not the other way around. As Peter described the interconnection: "in the meantime you are guarded by the power of God operating *through your faith*" (1 Peter 1). Our collective, individual belief is the channel chosen by Jesus for the flowing of the power of the Kingdom of Heaven into the world around us. And oh! how He *longs* to pipeline that power into our midst!

YOUR CONCLUSIONS:

IV.

ATTRACTIVE & ACCEPTING
EXHIBITING A "KINDNESS THAT LEADS TO REPENTANCE"

In the Roman world, the Early Church gatherings were a complete anomaly, a source of great wonderment, because of the spirit of love and life and joy radiating from their hearts. Those hearts were beating in time with the heart of Jesus Himself. These people would come together with power, miracles, healings, love and acceptance that were like Kingdom-of-Heaven-beacons amidst the darkness of the Empire. Their presence alone, with the Holy Spirit present within their hearts, was often enough to draw curious crowds of people to come and watch. Here's how the first 3,000 men and women happened to join their ranks:

> *"Then Peter stood up with the Eleven, raised his voice and addressed the crowd [who had gathered, curious, due to the Pentecost outpouring of the Holy Spirit]: 'Fellow Jews and all of you who live in Jerusalem, let me explain this to you; listen carefully to what I say…' With many other words he warned them; and he pleaded with them, 'Save yourselves from this corrupt generation.' Those who accepted his message were baptized, and about three thousand were added to their number that day." (Acts 2)*

It can be safely said that, had the Holy Spirit *not* been involved that day, *not* made His radical incursion into the Eleven, that nothing much might've happened. It can also be safely said that, had the Eleven *not* let forth with the gift of tongues, *not* proclaimed the name of Jesus, it would've been like any other day in Jerusalem.

Instead, in complete subjection to the power and glory and gifts of the Holy Spirit, the Eleven let loose with a torrent of His wondrous undeniable presence. And crowds of people couldn't *help* but be attracted to their fellowship. They simply *had* to see what was happening within this group of people.

Don't we long to see that same curious wonderment taking possession of people's hearts because of the power of Jesus alive at the core of our lives? Don't we dream of watching hundreds of hardened hearts, millions of closed minds, opened by the inexplicable incursions of the Holy Spirit and, by Him, Jesus?

Then we must *lead* with His power that unsettles and attracts. We must move *off* the measurable, scalable strategies that have been embraced so long. We must let loose of the ways we try to coax outsiders through the doors; we must allow His Holy Spirit to set the tone for *His* sort of attraction.

Because, really, the most attractive thing about the Church is Jesus Himself; you and I must better learn to let Him have His way, in and through us. And His way, by the way, is to be "lifted up" and to draw **"all men"** to Himself (John 12) – a seemingly blanket statement that He really and truly means:

> [Immediately after his conversion from antagonist to apostle on the road to Damascus:] *"Saul spent several days with the disciples in Damascus." (Acts 9)*

You see, not only did Jesus want Saul to stop persecuting, to come be His disciple and apostle, to write nearly a quarter of what we call the New Testament, He also wanted the Early Church to accept *him*. Imagine the challenge of accepting a man who recently wanted you dead! Indeed, there were some who questioned whether it was wise – or even safe:

> *"When [Saul] came to Jerusalem, he tried to join the disciples,*

THE LANTERN OUT OF DOORS

but they were all afraid of him, not believing that he really was a disciple. But Barnabas took him and brought him to the apostles. He told them how Saul on his journey had seen the Lord and that the Lord had spoken to him, and how in Damascus he had preached fearlessly in the name of Jesus. So Saul stayed with them and moved about freely in Jerusalem, speaking boldly in the name of the Lord." (Acts 9)

It was perfectly natural that the brothers and sisters in Jerusalem would question the intelligence of letting a murderous persecutor worship within their gathering. Especially a murderous persecutor who'd been murdering and persecuting *them!* Yet, just for this moment, they must have forgotten how disinterested Jesus generally was in almost anything that could be described as "perfectly natural." *His* acceptance of people was perfectly *un*natural. And so must it be for any gathering who calls upon His name.

Yet how, we might ask, are we to properly teach and correct the inherent waywardness and sinfulness in the hearts of the people who are *new* to the fellowship? The Early Church gatherings allowed the Lord Jesus Himself to take care of that:

"Many of those who believed now came and openly confessed what they had done. A number who had practiced sorcery brought their scrolls together and burned them publicly. When they calculated the value of the scrolls, the total came to fifty thousand drachmas. In this way the word of the Lord spread widely and grew in power." (Acts 19)

But what if we don't see such an immediate "open confession" of sin? What should we do if sin is unconfessed, yet obvious?

"Brothers and sisters, if someone is caught in a sin, you who live by the Spirit should restore that person gently. But watch

yourselves, or you also may be tempted. Carry each other's burdens, and in this way you will fulfill the law of Christ."
(Galatians 6)

The Early Church gatherings were not a people defined by sin; they were defined by the life and love and grace and invitation of Jesus. When measured against His perfection, people confessed their sin freely. And when they didn't, they were "restored gently" by people who loved them.

CONCLUSION: It's the presence of Jesus, the power of His love, the perfection of His character, that attracts outsiders, creates desire, and convicts the human heart of sin. No churchly contrivance can ever match His hand upon a life. Nothing we can ever do can merit mention alongside *His* Way.

The Early Church gatherings didn't grow because the "teaching there was so good," the children's programs were the best, the worship was stylish, or because the building they met in was modern, inviting. The Early Church gatherings attracted people because *He* was there. Even people like Saul – a murderous, unhinged, hateful sort of villain – were included and invited and accepted into the midst of the gathering. It was the job of the Holy Spirit to convict such people of sin. It was the gathering's job to "lift up" Jesus alone.

YOUR CONCLUSIONS:

V.

PRACTICAL

Something beautiful about the Early Church gatherings is just how practical they were; how they lived their belief sensibly and straightforwardly. Yes, they *absolutely* gave their hearts to the things of the Kingdom of Heaven, lived as if "raised up and seated in the heavenly places in Christ Jesus" (Ephesians 2:6), embraced the all-powerful presence of the Holy Spirit; and yet they did all these things in the context of the real world. They made simple decisions like all of us do. They continued to work and eat and raise families like we do. Yet, throughout it all, their practicality was infused with the climate and atmosphere of Heaven; they were truly living in both places at once.

Again, let's look at the famous descriptions from Acts 2:

> *"They devoted themselves to the apostles' teaching and to fellowship, to the breaking of bread and to prayer. Everyone was filled with awe at the many wonders and signs performed by the apostles. All the believers were together and had everything in common. They sold property and possessions to give to anyone who had need. Every day they continued to meet together in the temple courts. They broke bread in their homes and ate together with glad and sincere hearts, praising God and enjoying the favor of all the people. And the Lord added to their number daily those who were being saved."*

In this study, we've already discussed the power of the teaching, the prayer, and the openness to "wonders and signs" that characterized the Early Church gatherings. But, practically speaking, what do we make of devotion to the fellowship, breaking bread together, sharing everything in common, selling our property and possessions so that no one feels any need? How might we co-opt the everyday nature of their gatherings, the meeting in the temple courts *and* in homes, the favor that foreran their fellowship and invited in outsiders? I raise these questions more for discussion than to lend my own answer. Yet these are the questions that, I think, most matter for our purposes.

In fact, reread that Acts 2 paragraph, asking Him for His direct insight, and then make some notes below on how we might practically implant its elements into the spirit of our gathering:

Now let's look at one of the most practical passages you could ever want for our purposes:

> *"When you come together, each of you has a hymn, or a word of instruction, a revelation, a tongue or an interpretation. Everything must be done so that the church may be built up. If*

anyone speaks in a tongue, two — or at the most three — should speak, one at a time, and someone must interpret. If there is no interpreter, the speaker should keep quiet in the church and speak to himself and to God. Two or three prophets should speak, and the others should weigh carefully what is said. And if a revelation comes to someone who is sitting down, the first speaker should stop. For you can all prophesy in turn so that everyone may be instructed and encouraged. The spirits of prophets are subject to the control of prophets. For God is not a God of disorder but of peace — as in all the congregations of the Lord's people." (1 Corinthians 14)

Paul's instructions here are so comprehensively helpful that they even extend to how you *arrive* at the gathering, ie. how you prepare your heart to show up. Allow me to sketch out how this passage would work, both individually and corporately:

1. When apart, each individual will seek the face of Jesus and receive from Him songs, words of instruction, direct revelation, a tongue or an interpretation. These are meant for the individual's personal growth in Jesus **and** for the gathering's.

2. Each individual comes to the gathering *ready to minister* to the others with what they've received from Jesus; *ready to "build up" the Body* with the voice and love of Jesus through them.

3. There should be an open-format portion of our time for people to share before the broader group – two or three in tongues (provided they have an interpreter)[1] and two or three "prophets" who will share a testimony, word or exhortation.[2] Paul (also

---

[1] There will be absolutely no tongues spoken before the broader group without a direct interpretation *from another person*. No questions asked on this point.

in 1 Corinthians 14) explains why there must be order amidst the tongues and prophecy:

> *"Anyone who speaks in a tongue edifies himself, but the one who prophesies edifies the church. I would like every one of you to speak in tongues, but I would rather have you prophesy. The one who prophesies is greater than the one who speaks in tongues, unless someone interprets, so that the church may be edified… For this reason the one who speaks in a tongue should pray that they may interpret what they say."*

4. After the tongue-speak and/or time of prophecy, there should be a time of hearing from the group: What did *they* hear? What corresponded with something they've heard Him say before? How can we draw closer to Jesus based upon the words and thoughts we've just received?

5. Everything that's offered in the "bringing something & sharing something" portion of our gathering must answer to the description that "everyone may be instructed and encouraged." We're not after strange, abstruse, potentially divisive sorts of esoteric thinking about Jesus. We want *Him*.

6. Throughout every portion of the gathering, from opening prayer to final prayer, we desire only the Lord's peace. Anything that seems to disorder will not be done again.

---

[2] We should consider carefully how we shepherd this time of sharing from multiple "prophetic" voices. Perhaps people could express their desire to share and then be heard out by two or more of the leaders, simply to ensure that the spirit of their "word" or interpretation will be beneficial for the "building up" of the whole gathering.

THE LANTERN OUT OF DOORS

One of the simplest practicalities that we see in the Early Church gatherings – consistency of location – is given to us quite early in Acts:

> *"And all the believers used to meet together in Solomon's Colonnade… Crowds gathered also from the towns around Jerusalem, bringing their sick and those tormented by impure spirits, and all of them were healed." (Acts 5)*

For the sake of both the regular members and the "crowds" who want to hear of Jesus, it's absolutely imperative that we're consistent in our place and time and openness to receive all. Not that the physical location needs to be as impressive as Solomon's Colonnade in Herod's Temple:

> *"Paul, a prisoner of Christ Jesus, and Timothy our brother, to Philemon our dear friend and fellow worker — also to Apphia our sister and Archippus our fellow soldier—and to the church* **that meets in your home***…" (The Letter to Philemon)*

Many of the Early Church gatherings chose to gather in the homes of their city's first believers, both probably for the intimacy engendered, as well as for the opportunity for hospitality.

A question for our consideration: If we *don't* choose to meet in a home, and instead meet in a larger central venue, what steps can we take to ensure that our gathering-place *feels* like a home?

Finally, we must touch on a Pauline practicality that will be the SINGLE AND ONLY EXCEPTION we take from the New Testament teachings about the Early Church gatherings. From 1 Corinthians 14:

> *"Women should remain silent in the churches. They are not*

> *allowed to speak, but must be in submission, as the law says. If they want to inquire about something, they should ask their own husbands at home; for it is disgraceful for a woman to speak in the church."*

We will *not* not follow this teaching because of modern feminism, or our discomfort with countercultural faith-practices, or for any other reason but this one: that Jesus Himself, in His *own* interaction with women, raised their status *far higher* than Paul would seem to allow for, here. In Ephesians 4, Paul describes the five main "offices" of the Church in this way: "He gave some to be *apostles*; and some, *prophets*; and some, *evangelists*; and some, *pastors* and *teachers*; for the perfecting of the saints, to the work of serving, to the building up of the body of Christ; until we all attain to the unity of the faith, and of the knowledge of the Son of God…"

When we consider Jesus' utilization of the gifts and faith of the women who accompanied Him, it's actually quite stunning how He not only normalized their presence and participation within His ministry, but actually exalted them to these five offices. Consider those roles and the various women He chose:

APOSTLE – Mary Magdalene, who is sent to tell the disciples about the Resurrection (John 20)

PROPHET – Jesus' mother, Mary, whose "Magnificat" is direct glorious prophecy about His ministry (Luke 1)

EVANGELIST – The Samaritan woman at the well, who goes and tells her whole town about the Messiah's arrival (John 4)

PASTOR – The group of women who provide for Jesus; for His monetary and daily needs (Luke 8)

TEACHER – Mary, the sister of Lazarus, whose faith very clearly teaches her own sister Martha how to approach Jesus (John 11)

For the reason of the example of Jesus, we are going to choose His way with women's leadership over Paul's exhortations from 1 Corinthians (as well as 1 Timothy 2). We don't need to denigrate the views of complementarian churches or fellowships; this is simply the choice we are making for our own gathering.

CONCLUSION: Our gathering must readily embrace the practicality and the smart, simple practices of the Early Church gatherings. From our discussion of that passage in Acts 2, to our format according to the sharing of tongues and prophets, to the location and consistency and duration of our times, to the sense of "home" we desire to create – all of it must lend itself to the peace of God and the creation of a gathering that points to Jesus alone. The exact details may shift and change over time, but not the non-negotiability of His presence being our highest goal together.

YOUR CONCLUSIONS:

VI.

INDIVISIBLE & FOCUSED ON UNITY
OPEN TO ALL THE GIFTS

Although we see disputes in the first generation of the
Early Church gatherings, we see no evidence of any sort of
major schism or general parting-of-ways. This is a miracle
– *and* a stark reminder of how intimately they walked with
Jesus. Rather than setting up camps, they would work
together quickly, whenever any kind of trouble arose, to
move back into unity with each other and with Jesus. They
wouldn't have been able to conceive of a Body that was
contentious, quarrelsome, apt to split. *How*, they would've
asked us, *can a Body be cut to pieces and live?*

1. Their eyes were on Jesus alone.

The only provenance for this wondrous, mystical unity was
that every single member of the gatherings kept their eyes
on Jesus alone. Listen to one of my favorite "toasts" to
Jesus, by the Apostle Paul:

> *"Now to him who is able to do immeasurably more than all we
> ask or imagine, according to his power that is at work within
> us, to him be glory in the church and in Christ Jesus throughout
> all generations, for ever and ever! Amen." (Ephesians 3)*

For Paul, to look on Jesus was to love Jesus, to learn His
immeasurable power, to glory in His goodness to the
church, and to know that nothing is impossible where He
presides. For us, we must first deliver up our doubts that
unity-in-the-Body is even *possible*; we must reckon with the
fact that few of us believe He *can* re-unify our countless
breaks.

Let it be understood: Jesus *demands* unity in His Body.
After all, it was His final prayer for us before He was

THE LANTERN OUT OF DOORS

arrested. You and I must first draw near to Him before we can even *attempt* to draw near to each other; the unity of the Church can only be forged from each individual's individual union with Jesus.

But oh! my friends, He *can* do it – He *will* do it:

> *"May the God who gives endurance and encouragement give you the same attitude of mind toward each other that Christ Jesus had, so that with one mind and one voice you may glorify the God and Father of our Lord Jesus Christ. Accept one another, then, just as Christ accepted you, in order to bring praise to God." (Romans 15)*

It's in the nature of God to ask us for something – in this case, that we would be one in Him – and then *bestow upon us* all the necessary means to accomplish that obedience. "The God who gives endurance and encouragement" in ever-abundant, always-endless measure is the very same One who desires to "*give you* the same attitude of mind toward each other that Christ Jesus had…" He wants to change our minds to *want* to be one with each other. Unity is a spiritual end that only *He* can give the means to reach.

But as we, individually, focus our hearts on Jesus and His asked-for unity in the church, consider the sort of spirit that breaks out within our fellowship:

> *"Let the peace of Christ rule in your hearts, since as members of one body you were called to peace. And be thankful. Let the message of Christ dwell among you richly as you teach and admonish one another with all wisdom through psalms, hymns, and songs from the Spirit, singing to God with gratitude in your hearts. And whatever you do, whether in word or deed, do it all in the name of the Lord Jesus, giving thanks to God the Father through him." (Colossians 3)*

Imagine arriving at a gathering where the peace of Christ

rules, where everyone is thankful, where the message of Jesus lives in the teaching, admonition, worship, and in every heart present. Do you think you'd have to do much to entice others to join? No, you'd instead see every individual losing himself in the presence of a Jesus who is *clearly* alive because He's so *clearly* present in the room, right that minute. Any visitor would have to wrestle – not with their preferences about worship, their liking of the pastor etc – but with the unbridled experience of experiencing Jesus first-hand.

So what's the first step toward this sort of unity? Our *leaders* must renounce themselves, looking to Jesus alone –

> *"I appeal to you, brothers and sisters, in the name of our Lord Jesus Christ, that all of you agree with one another in what you say and that there be no divisions among you, but that you be perfectly united in mind and thought. My brothers and sisters, some from Chloe's household have informed me that there are quarrels among you. What I mean is this: One of you says, 'I follow Paul'; another, 'I follow Apollos'; another, 'I follow Cephas'; still another, 'I follow Christ.' Is Christ divided? Was Paul crucified for you? Were you baptized in the name of Paul?" (1 Corinthians 1)*

If our leaders are prepared to take *no* credit, *no* special position, *no* privilege, *no* "cult of personality" status, we will be off on the right path toward being "perfectly united." Our leaders must be leaders, first, in complete self-abnegation. Only Jesus is allowed to stick His head up above the crowd.

2. They saw themselves as His Body *exactly – together.*

What's become most stunning to me about the comprisal of the Early Church gatherings is how completely they believed that they were *actually* the Body of Christ. *Literally*

THE LANTERN OUT OF DOORS

Jesus. For them, the "Body" wasn't some ancient theological idea, some clever spiritual-sounding construct, they – together – worked to form a unity that *was* Him. Again, not figuratively. They believed it *literally*. Take a look at Paul's familiar words that paint the picture so well:

> *"For just as each of us has one body with many members, and these members do not all have the same function, so in Christ we, though many, form one body, and each member belongs to all the others. We have different gifts, according to the grace given to each of us. If your gift is prophesying, then prophesy in accordance with your faith; if it is serving, then serve; if it is teaching, then teach; if it is to encourage, then give encouragement; if it is giving, then give generously; if it is to lead, do it diligently; if it is to show mercy, do it cheerfully."* (Romans 12)

Just as his readers could glance from the written word to the flesh and bones they personally inhabited – *just like that!* – they were meant to view their lives within the Christ-Body context. The different "members" played a part that was just as distinct, just as integral, as the part that the members of their own physical body played to keep the whole functioning. He continues the theme in 1 Corinthians 12:

> *"Now to each one the manifestation of the Spirit is given for the common good. To one there is given through the Spirit a message of wisdom, to another a message of knowledge by means of the same Spirit, to another faith by the same Spirit, to another gifts of healing by that one Spirit, to another miraculous powers, to another prophecy, to another distinguishing between spirits, to another speaking in different kinds of tongues, and to still another the interpretation of tongues. All these are the work of one and the same Spirit, and he distributes them to each one, just as he determines. Just as a body, though one, has many parts, but all its many parts form one body, so it is with Christ. For we were all baptized by one*

Spirit so as to form one body."

What a miracle that, before the foundations of the creation of the world, He could choose such different, disparate individuals as you and me to become the members who would recreate His Body. And to think He's able to do it in every successive generation! His wisdom truly knows no bounds, no limits!

And I don't think I'd be taking too much poetic or theological license to say that the "blood" that feeds and fuels the Body's life is the "one Spirit" – the Holy Spirit. As the blood is presently flowing through your own body while you're reading these words, nourishing, enlivening, connecting into unity, *so* the Holy Spirit nourishes, enlivens and connects us, one to another.

3. The Body Functions *by* the Gifts

The most dangerous threat to the Body isn't infection by a strain of bad theology, outside attack by Satan, or, as is presently the source of great concern in the American Church, dwindling numbers. The greatest threat are the members who cease to function *as* members. When individuals begin to view themselves as unnecessary, redundant, ungifted, or "not a part," they draw back into an unhealthy spiritual introversion that thwarts their growth – *and* the Body's.

The need? That *each* would believe in the giftings of the Holy Spirit and – just as importantly – actually know the gifting they've *each* received, in order to properly function within, and serve, the Body. Look at how clearly the first Apostles knew the part they were meant to play:

"So the Twelve gathered all the disciples together and said, 'It would not be right for us to neglect the ministry of the word of God in order to wait on tables. Brothers and sisters, choose

THE LANTERN OUT OF DOORS

seven men from among you who are known to be full of the Spirit and wisdom. We will turn this responsibility [of caring for the widows] over to them and will give our attention to prayer and the ministry of the word.' This proposal pleased the whole group." (Acts 6)

Because they'd each received the "ministry of the word" directly from the hand of Jesus, the Twelve simply refused to do anything that might interfere with the specificity of that calling. They didn't confuse diffuse busyness for Kingdom-fruitfulness. Instead, by sticking to the gifting for which they'd originally been called, they opened opportunity for the first seven deacons to minister within their *own* given gifting. In the gathering at Antioch, we see the same sort of differentiation occurring:

"Then Barnabas went to Tarsus to look for Saul, and when he found him, he brought him to Antioch. So for a whole year Barnabas and Saul met with the church and taught great numbers of people. The disciples were called Christians first at Antioch. During this time some prophets came down from Jerusalem to Antioch. One of them, named Agabus, stood up and through the Spirit predicted that a severe famine would spread over the entire Roman world. (This happened during the reign of Claudius.) The disciples, as each one was able, decided to provide help for the brothers and sisters living in Judea. This they did, sending their gift to the elders by Barnabas and Saul." (Acts 11)

It was because the teachers *only* taught and the prophets *only* prophesied that the gathering in Antioch was spurred toward this collective generosity for the church in Judea. In fact, a heartfelt generous spirit is what both animates *and* results from the proper experience and service of the giftings of the Holy Spirit:

"Offer hospitality to one another without grumbling. Each of you should use whatever gift you have received to serve others, as

41

faithful stewards of God's grace in its various forms. If anyone speaks, they should do so as one who speaks the very words of God. If anyone serves, they should do so with the strength God provides, so that in all things God may be praised through Jesus Christ." (1 Peter 4)

Each of us has a Gift that's meant to be used to serve the Body. Our knowing that Gift and being useful with it is absolutely imperative. When you consider the following list that Paul relates in 1 Corinthians 12, where does the Holy Spirit cause *your* heart to say, "Yes, that one's *me*"?

"Now you are the body of Christ, and each one of you is a part of it. And God has placed in the church first of all apostles, second prophets, third teachers, then miracles, then gifts of healing, of helping, of guidance, and of different kinds of tongues."

Which of those roles seems like its yours? Make a note to yourself here:

The Body of Christ can only function in its proper, alive, active, miraculous ways when *each of us* lives from the gifting He has purposely placed within us. If any of us doesn't know our gifting, we must come to know it immediately. If any of us knows yet doesn't *pursue* it, they must cease to do so. We must *each one of us* grasp the reason for which we were chosen and called to the Body; we must *each one of us* exercise the fullness of that Gift on behalf of the Body.

And in order to ensure our being spurred together forever in that direction, He also appointed within the gatherings a five-headed leadership team:

"So Christ himself gave the apostles, the prophets, the evangelists, the pastors and teachers, to equip his people for works of service, so that the body of Christ may be built up until we all reach unity in the faith and in the knowledge of the Son of God and become mature, attaining to the whole measure of the fullness of Christ. Then we will no longer be infants, tossed back and forth by the waves, and blown here and there by every wind of teaching and by the cunning and craftiness of people in their deceitful scheming. Instead, speaking the truth in love, we will grow to become in every respect the mature body of him who is the head, that is, Christ. From him the whole body, joined and held together by every supporting ligament, grows and builds itself up in love, as each part does its work." (Ephesians 4)

Did you catch the purpose for which the leadership of the gathering must include all five types of leaders – Apostles, Prophets, Evangelists, Pastors and Teachers? Read it again: "**so that** the body of Christ may be built up until we all reach unity in the faith and in the knowledge of the Son of God and become mature, attaining to the whole measure of the fullness of Christ."

In other words, if the gathering *doesn't* have a co-equal, five-headed leadership team, comprised of Apostles, Prophets, Evangelists, Pastors and Teachers, we will *not* be built up into unity, we will *not* grow in the knowledge of the Son of God, we will *not* become mature and attain to the whole measure of the fullness of Christ. All five types of leaders are absolutely necessary. None can ever be dismissed.

4. When disagreements arose within the Early Church

Before we can even begin to study how the gatherings dealt with their conflicts, strife and disagreement, we must first consider the sort of spirit that perpetually lived in their hearts. Paul points to it by making the following exhortations:

> *"Therefore let us stop passing judgment on one another. Instead, make up your mind not to put any stumbling block or obstacle in the way of a brother or sister... So whatever you believe about these things [regarding food and drink] keep between yourself and God. Blessed is the one who does not condemn himself by what he approves." (Romans 14)*

The Early Church gatherings were filled with people so consumed with Jesus, so busy in the service of His Kingdom, that we can imagine they simply sloughed off most of their disagreements before they really arose. They lived as people who were "making up their minds" to not present a stumbling block to others, and they consciously worked to rid their minds of judgment-of-others. Just think of how much freedom we're granted in those twin commands!

And, too, look how quickly Paul diminished lesser behavioral questions that, today, would be turned into theological factions and around which battling denominations would form:

> *"One person considers one day more sacred than another; another considers every day alike. Each of them should be fully convinced in their own mind. Whoever regards one day as special does so to the Lord. Whoever eats meat does so to the Lord, for they give thanks to God; and whoever abstains does so to the Lord and gives thanks to God. For none of us lives for ourselves alone, and none of us dies for ourselves alone. If we live, we live for the Lord; and if we die, we die for the Lord. So, whether we live or die, we belong to the Lord." (Romans 14)*

When we consider the magnitude of the life and death of Jesus, when we realize the immensity of the call upon His Body, most else simply fades away. If we are committed to the Great Commission, abiding in the glories of the

mysteries of Abiding-in-Him, we simply won't have time –
or make time – for contentiousness. In fact:

> *"Don't have anything to do with foolish and stupid arguments,
> because you know they produce quarrels. And the Lord's
> servant must not be quarrelsome but must be kind to everyone,
> able to teach, not resentful. Opponents must be gently
> instructed, in the hope that God will grant them repentance
> leading them to a knowledge of the truth, and that they will
> come to their senses and escape from the trap of the devil, who
> has taken them captive to do his will." (2 Timothy 2)*

Isn't it fascinating that Timothy is *not* told to better his
theological arguments, nor to hone his razor-sharp
intellect, but instead is to "gently instruct" his opponents
with a view to their repentance? Oh, what heartache the
Church would avoid if such gentleness was first and
foremost!

But, we ask, what about when a true division arises? How
should we proceed when there is the real and open
potential for a real and open division within the gathering?

Let's consider the exact path that the Early Church trod in
such a case:

> *Certain people came down from Judea to Antioch and were
> teaching the believers: 'Unless you are circumcised, according to
> the custom taught by Moses, you cannot be saved.' This brought
> Paul and Barnabas into sharp dispute and debate with them.
> So Paul and Barnabas were appointed, along with some other
> believers, to go up to Jerusalem to see the apostles and elders
> about this question." (Acts 15)*

There's *no question* that "this question" had every earthly
potential to be enormously divisive; this could've been the
early end of the Early Church's complete unity. However,
Paul and Barnabas, rather than devolving into a series of

"sharp disputes," instead immediately sought to seek the counsel of the first Apostles in Jerusalem. And it wasn't as if Paul was remotely neutral about this topic! Hear how passionate was his regard for, and his protectiveness of, the Gentiles in the gathering's midst:

> *"When Cephas [later on] came to Antioch, I opposed him to his face, because he stood condemned. For before certain men came from James, he used to eat with the Gentiles. But when they arrived, he began to draw back and separate himself from the Gentiles because he was afraid of those who belonged to the circumcision group. The other Jews joined him in his hypocrisy, so that by their hypocrisy even Barnabas was led astray. When I saw that they were not acting in line with the truth of the gospel, I said to Cephas in front of them all, 'You are a Jew, yet you live like a Gentile and not like a Jew. How is it, then, that you force Gentiles to follow Jewish customs?'" (Galatians 2)*

Now imagine Paul and Barnabas traveling to Jerusalem with the fate of the church's unity hanging on this question of Gentile circumcision. With fire in their eyes, and coming right on the heels of the experiences of their first missionary journey, they come to state their viewpoint before the assembled Elders. Which, actually, raises a good point for our consideration:

> *"Then some of the believers who belonged to the party of the Pharisees stood up and said, 'The Gentiles must be circumcised and required to keep the law of Moses.' The apostles and elders met to consider this question." (Acts 15)*

Before Paul and Barnabas speak, they let their opponents speak. Each "side" was allowed to state their case with clarity. Then, after listening, Paul and Barnabas take their turn and, then, pay attention for who speaks directly after them:

THE LANTERN OUT OF DOORS

"The whole assembly became silent as they listened to Barnabas and Paul telling about the signs and wonders God had done among the Gentiles through them. When they finished, James spoke up. 'Brothers,' he said, 'listen to me....'" (Acts 15)

It was deeply important for the Early Church gatherings to have wise, mature, steadfast leaders who could "speak the truth in love" to the others. James (most likely the James who was the brother of Jesus Himself) here listened to both sides of the controversy and then, with a calm spirit, rose to address the gathering. The eventual resolution was the fruit of his listening ear. *And* of the others' ability, and humility, to be led by him.

So, upon the occasion of a disagreement, dispute, controversy, theological question or interpersonal issue arising, we will follow the Early Church gatherings in the exact steps they pursued:

1. When such an issue is raised, it is immediately confronted and addressed.

2. A council of trusted brothers and sisters is convened for its consideration.

3. Both sides of the issue are allowed to present their individual viewpoints.

4. One or more Elder is allowed to speak about the controversy with insight added.

5. A decision is reached with which both the leaders and the gathering *will* agree.

It's imperative, however, that everyone in the gathering would approach such a potentially divisive moment with their eyes fixed on Jesus alone, not on the issue itself. Historically, focus on "theological issues" has tended to exalt individuals and individual viewpoints above Jesus; the

Body-context is, in that manner, quickly forgotten.

But brothers and sisters who will settle for nothing less than His uniting presence *together* are able to weather such storms *together*, borne along by the waves of His love and grace *together*. That's why Paul was so blunt about steering clear of perpetual dividers:

> *"I urge you, brothers and sisters, to watch out for those who cause divisions and put obstacles in your way that are contrary to the teaching you have learned. Keep away from them."*
> *(Romans 16)*

And in a case where an individual was "uncorrectable" and persistently a fractious influence upon the gathering, here was the seriousness with which Paul instructed the Corinthians:

> *"So when you are assembled and I am with you in spirit, and the power of our Lord Jesus is present, hand this man over to Satan for the destruction of the flesh, so that his spirit may be saved on the day of the Lord." (1 Corinthians 5)*

5. The Early Church gatherings were enamored with Jesus, with each other, and with their unbelievably high calling to be His Body.

In the midst of all their movements and miracles, the Early Church gatherings were undergirded by love – love for Jesus, love for each other, and a shared love of the impossible glories to which they'd together been called. They would happily go out of their way to extend the love of Jesus to each other; they knew how far "out of His way" Jesus had come for each of *them*. They were delighted to extend the love of Jesus practically, one to another, and the world around them was changed by witnessing such a love in action. Here's just one example of a gathering extending its heart:

THE LANTERN OUT OF DOORS

"We sought out the disciples [in Tyre] and stayed with them seven days. Through the Spirit they urged Paul not to go on to Jerusalem. When it was time to leave, we left and continued on our way. All of them, including wives and children, accompanied us out of the city, and there on the beach we knelt to pray." (Acts 21)

Because they were so spread out across the Roman world, the Early Church gatherings looked for every opportunity to share experiences, fellowship and, also, what they were learning. They weren't afraid to even imitate each other when they saw certain gatherings excelling in the work of the Lord – look at how the Thessalonians copied those who worshipped in Judea:

"For you, brothers and sisters, became imitators of God's churches in Judea, which are in Christ Jesus." (1 Thessalonians 2)

But in order to humble themselves and learn the Way of Jesus from each other, it was absolutely necessary that – *together* – they understand the glories of their joint calling. For us, if we are – *together* – to attempt to emulate the Early Church gatherings, we must also understand the glories of that unchanging, still-the-same calling on us:

"As you come to him, the living Stone — rejected by humans but chosen by God and precious to him — you also, like living stones, are being built into a spiritual house to be a holy priesthood, offering spiritual sacrifices acceptable to God through Jesus Christ… But you are a chosen people, a royal priesthood, a holy nation, God's special possession, that you may declare the praises of him who called you out of darkness into his wonderful light. Once you were not a people, but now you are the people of God; once you had not received mercy, but now you have received mercy." (1 Peter 2)

Brothers and Sisters, we *together* comprise the "spiritual

house" of God **and**, *together*, we are the "holy priesthood" ministering therein. *Together*, the Spirit-in-us envelops the whole world in His Presence and, *together*, we are daily recreating the visible, tangible Body of Christ. What a high and joyous calling is ours – *together!*

CONCLUSION: **Jesus has specifically chosen individuals like us to be spiritually united by Him into a cohesive unit that actually *is* Him – His "Body." This Body attains its unity only by keeping its eyes on Him, operating from the giftings of His Holy Spirit, and by settling for nothing less than a complete oneness. When issues arise between us, constructive steps must immediately be taken, and yet the focus on unity can never flag: a Body cannot be split and live. We must accept and live from the fullness of our calling *together*. We must pursue Him *together* or we can't attain to His fullness.**

YOUR CONCLUSIONS:

VII

LED BY SHEPHERDS WHO BORE THE STAMP OF JESUS

The leaders of the first generation of the Early Church gatherings received their calling to lead from the hand of Jesus – even if they'd never personally met Him. So apparent was His presence, so alive His power in the hearts of the assembled brothers and sisters, that the next ones chosen sensed no difference between themselves and the Apostles. The same must still be true for our leaders today. When the voice of Jesus calls a man or woman to lead within His Body, that is the first and most important prequalification necessary. The rest – the character needed, the spirit engendered, the vision for the lives of others – can only follow from a direct intimacy with Jesus Himself.

Listen to how Paul exhorted the assemblage of Elders from the Ephesian gathering:

> *"Keep watch over yourselves and all the flock of which the Holy Spirit has made you overseers. Be shepherds of the church of God, which he bought with his own blood." (Acts 20)*

A leader's self-perception must be anchored in their awareness that they are a shepherd specifically chosen by *the* Good Shepherd (John 10) to carefully care for the flock "which he bought with his own blood." Any lesser view is not only unhelpful, it can be disastrous. Diminishing the call of the leader diminishes the destiny of the gathering.

But what is entailed in being a "shepherd" of people? Peter explains:

> *"To the elders among you, I appeal as a fellow elder and a witness of Christ's sufferings who also will share in the glory to be revealed: Be shepherds of God's flock that is under your care, watching over them — not because you must, but because you*

are willing, as God wants you to be; not pursuing dishonest gain, but eager to serve; not lording it over those entrusted to you, but being examples to the flock. And when the Chief Shepherd appears, you will receive the crown of glory that will never fade away." (1 Peter 5)

Any man or woman who senses the calling to shepherd the Body must *already* exhibit the sort of spirit to which Peter points in those words. Consider those attributes again, listed out:

1. A watchful care for others

2. A sacrificial willingness to lead

3. Honesty in all matters

4. Eager, at all times, to serve

5. Humble and gentle

6. A steadfast example of the love and life of Jesus

7. A life lived confidently under the gaze of Jesus

To see the practical application of those characteristics, take a look at Paul and Barnabas in Acts 14:

"They preached the gospel in that city (Derbe) and won a large number of disciples. Then they returned to Lystra, Iconium and Antioch, strengthening the disciples and encouraging them to remain true to the faith. 'We must go through many hardships to enter the kingdom of God,' they said. Paul and Barnabas appointed elders for them in each church and, with prayer and fasting, committed them to the Lord, in whom they had put their trust."

They weren't only traveling and teaching; Paul and Barnabas were conscientiously shepherding each of the

THE LANTERN OUT OF DOORS

flocks they themselves had first established in that region. Their care for their people called for strengthening and encouraging, for honest-speaking, for prayer, and for helping to choose the leaders who would then succeed them there in ministry. This generational style of succession was taught to Timothy too:

> *"You then, my son, be strong in the grace that is in Christ Jesus. And the things you have heard me say in the presence of many witnesses entrust to reliable people who will also be qualified to teach others." (2 Timothy 2)*

Timothy's shepherding of his flock depended solely upon his own personal dependence upon the strength that's found in the grace that's found in Jesus alone. And, like Paul had done with him, he was then instructed to identify the *next* generation of potential leadership and pass that first-hand knowledge along, along with the stamp of Christ's authority.

As we ourselves assemble a team of leaders to shepherd our flock, let us consider the qualifications Paul had earlier written down for Timothy:

> *"Now the overseer is to be above reproach, faithful to his wife, temperate, self-controlled, respectable, hospitable, able to teach, not given to drunkenness, not violent but gentle, not quarrelsome, not a lover of money. He must manage his own family well and see that his children obey him, and he must do so in a manner worthy of full respect. (If anyone does not know how to manage his own family, how can he take care of God's church?) He must not be a recent convert, or he may become conceited and fall under the same judgment as the devil. He must also have a good reputation with outsiders, so that he will not fall into disgrace and into the devil's trap. In the same way, deacons are to be worthy of respect, sincere, not indulging in much wine, and not pursuing dishonest gain. They must keep hold of the deep truths of the faith with a clear conscience. They*

must first be tested; and then if there is nothing against them, let them serve as deacons." (1 Timothy 3)

This lengthy list was not provided to Timothy as some sort of "best case scenario," or as wishful thinking about the kind of people Paul *hoped* he would find. These are the actual qualities *required* for leadership in the Body.

In the Modern Church, we often find people in positions of leadership simply because they were initially willing to give their time away, or because a position simply needed filling. They are, of course, to be applauded for desiring to serve the Body.

But Paul would *never* have approved of a choice that was based on scarcity. No, knowing Paul, he probably would've said that having *no* leaders was infinitely preferable to lessening the quality of the leaders in the Body's service. It's clear how highly he viewed the role, based on the following:

"Do not entertain an accusation against an elder unless it is brought by two or three witnesses. But those elders who are sinning you are to reprove before everyone, so that the others may take warning." (1 Timothy 5)

Chosen leaders are to be held in the highest regard and, as Paul says, it will require more than just a single casual charge against them to remove them from their service. However, it should also be a strong warning to every potential leader within the gathering just how *sternly* Paul called for their censure, should the charge be proven to be true.

CONCLUSION: **Leadership in the Early Church gatherings was a calling directly from Jesus; the leaders were viewed as shepherds called by *the* Good Shepherd. We must look for the same call and the** same heart in our leaders. They must be people who *currently* answer to the descriptions offered up in Paul's instructions to Timothy; leadership in the gathering is not the staging ground to *learn* leadership. We're looking for people whose natural intimacy with Jesus creates a teachable, teaching spirit that attracts all people they meet to Him alone.

YOUR CONCLUSIONS:

VIII.

ENCOURAGED BY, AND ENCOURAGING WITH, THE SPIRIT OF JESUS

The word "encourage" is built from the prefix "en-" and the Old French word "corage," which itself is derived from the Latin for heart – "cor." To "encourage" thus means to "put in, or make, heart." What a perfect description of the Early Church gatherings! These were *literally* men and women whose hearts had been so utterly changed and made new by the love of Jesus that it was as if their old hearts had been removed and replaced. Jesus had now put in a new heart – *His* heart. The spirit of His encouragement now ruled and reigned in their collective midst.

Look at how conscientiously Paul considered how he might make sure that each of the churches in one of his circuits might be encouraged in the Lord:

> *"Give my greetings to the brothers and sisters at Laodicea, and to Nympha and the church in her house. After this letter has been read to you, see that it is also read in the church of the Laodiceans and that you in turn read the letter from Laodicea." (Colossians 4)*

How important it was to him that the separated gatherings of the Early Church should all be deeply encouraged by the direct love of Jesus for each of them. Otherwise, how could they encourage the world around them?

For the same reason, how important it *is* that the separated individuals who will convene at our gathering should be deeply encouraged by the direct love of Jesus for *them*. Otherwise, how will they encourage the world around us? We must, like Paul, have a mind that's bent on creating a constant spirit of encouragement.

So from where will such a spirit of encouragement first spring up? Again, it's from the hearts of leaders whose *own* hearts are encouraged by Jesus:

> *"After Paul and Silas came out of the prison, they went to Lydia's house, where they met with the brothers and sisters and encouraged them. Then they left." (Acts 16)*

Imagine the courage it took to enter prison for the sake of the Gospel of Jesus; now imagine the courage it took to exit and then encourage *others*. Paul and Silas weren't giving away a stream of something they didn't personally possess; they were diverting the encouraging spirit of Jesus *through* themselves to others. Having only just been imprisoned, threatened with torture and possibly death, they were easily able to redirect the encouragement of the Lord upon this small Philippian gathering. Later, we will see this same activity redirected toward them:

> *"The brothers and sisters [in Rome] had heard that we were coming, and they traveled as far as the Forum of Appius and the Three Taverns to meet us. At the sight of these people Paul thanked God and was encouraged." (Acts 28)*

As the leaders of the gathering encourage, so the led will encourage. As the spirit of the gathering goes, so will go its members. One of the primary reasons for which a gathering gathers is that all who walk through the doors might be overwhelmed by Jesus' goodness, faithfulness and His power that cannot help but encourage:

> *"On arriving [to Antioch], they gathered the church together and reported all that God had done through them and how he had opened a door of faith to the Gentiles." (Acts 14)*

This is why the "open-format portion" of our time is going to be so important – it allows for various voices to give testimony to His ongoing glorious work in the world.

It "puts heart into" our hearts to hear the specifics and logistics for how His variegated ways are expressing themselves through, and in the midst of, our scattered, very different lives. And look at how that spirit of encouragement flows back and forth through the Body:

> *"When we arrived at Jerusalem, the brothers and sisters received us warmly. The next day Paul and the rest of us went to see James, and all the elders were present. Paul greeted them and reported in detail what God had done among the Gentiles through his ministry. When they heard this, they praised God."*
> *(Acts 21)*

The Jerusalem gathering received Paul "warmly" and encouragingly, and Paul, the very next day, warmed their hearts and encouraged their spirits with the stories of how far the Gospel was going. Imagine that moment. The fellowship in Jerusalem, the place where all this originally started, is now receiving with open arms the man who once had hunted them down. And both sides, in turn, are encouraging and encouraged by each other. Truly, encouragement begets encouragement in Christ's Body.

But what about when the circumstances we face together are far from encouraging? What about when the hearts within the fellowship are far from each other?

Let's look back now at how that divisive moment we discussed in Chapter VI ended up being resolved within the space of that one Biblical chapter:

> *"So the men [from the Jerusalem council] were sent off and went down to Antioch, where they gathered the church together and delivered the letter. The people read it and were glad for its encouraging message. Judas and Silas, who themselves were prophets, said much to encourage and strengthen the believers. After spending some time there, they were sent off by the believers with the blessing of peace to return to those who had*

THE LANTERN OUT OF DOORS

sent them. But Paul and Barnabas remained in Antioch, where they and many others taught and preached the word of the Lord." (Acts 15)

Now let's be reminded of the variables that opened the events of Acts 15:

1. After a fruitful first missionary journey, Paul and Barnabas, only just arriving back at Antioch, were confronted with the issue of Gentile circumcision.

2. Bitter controversy ensued.

3. Paul and Barnabas, along with the men on the other side of the dispute, traveled to Jerusalem to consult the Apostles and Elders there.

4. The opposition stated their case.

5. Peter reminded the gathering of the story of Cornelius, a Gentile, receiving salvation in the name of Jesus.

6. Paul and Barnabas testified to the movement of the Holy Spirit amongst other uncircumcised Gentiles.

7. James, after having considered both sides, stated a final position that the Elders would take.

8. As we just read, the final "verdict" encouraged the people in Antioch.

It's not too much to say that, when a minor dispute troubles the serenity of a modern-day congregation, the last thing people expect is a conclusion of encouragement. Really, the high bar of hope is just that people won't leave in anger. Yet here's the Early Church dealing with a dispute that centers around *thousands of years of religious*

59

tradition and yet, within one chapter, they've already arrived at mutual encouragement. Judas and Silas are both prophesying again; Paul and Barnabas are back to their teaching; no one seems to miss a beat in the cycle of encouragement.

Which brings us to the final thought in this section – how the rhythms of the Body's encouragement demand consistency, constancy, concurrency:

> *"See to it, brothers and sisters, that none of you has a sinful, unbelieving heart that turns away from the living God. But encourage one another daily, as long as it is called 'Today,' so that none of you may be hardened by sin's deceitfulness. We have come to share in Christ, if indeed we hold our original conviction firmly to the very end." (Hebrews 3)*

Consider the logic of that passage from back to front. If we together firmly hold our original convictions, we will share in the life of Christ, unbothered by sin's deceitfulness, because we're daily encouraged, as brothers and sisters, to believe and stay in step with Him. In other words, one of our most basic needs is a daily dose of each other!

Together, let's pray for insight into how – **specifically** – the "Today" nature of encouragement might come to typify the way we interact with each other. We'll consider that more in the next chapter as well.

CONCLUSION: The Early Church gatherings were a people encouraged by, and encouraging others with, the direct encouraging spirit of Jesus. They always lived by His encouragement and were led by people who encouraged them deeply, just as He Himself had encouraged His own disciples.

Let us always consider – *before* and *after* any time we

THE LANTERN OUT OF DOORS

gather – whether that encouraging/encouraged spirit has both welcomed-in and also sent out our brothers and sisters. Heavy-heartedness was not in evidence in the Early Church. And it should never be a fruit of our present gatherings in His Name.

YOUR CONCLUSIONS:

IX.

THEY GATHERED TOGETHER CONSTANTLY

Since we collectively are not only the Body of Christ, but also His long-awaited Bride, let's extend that latter image further for this chapter's purposes. Imagine a beautiful bride and a handsome groom. For months, they've been planning every detail of their wedding day – all the sights, sounds, smells and tastes – and they've been spending lavishly from the resources of the groom's father. They cannot *wait* to arrive upon the day when everything will change; when the world will see their union affirmed, their commitment confessed, their love consummated.

Finally that day arrives. Hosts of well-dressed guests descend upon the beautiful venue chosen by the bride and groom and, by his consent, the father; everyone rejoices in the young couple's joy. The ceremony is followed by a lavish reception – all is delight and laughter and dancing and celebration of love in all its glorious splendor. The young couple leaves, now husband and wife. Everyone sighs a sigh of hopeful well-wishing, watching them go…

That couple then, once a week (sometimes a little less, depending upon their extremely busy schedule), meet each other for a formal show of "love," each Sunday morning. The rest of each week, they are always free to pursue their own purposes. They continue on in this ever-waning love-routine for a little over fifty years, get older, retire from life, and then die.

Would you call that a love story? I think not.

The Early Church gatherings, as the acknowledged, delighted, bursting-with-joy Bride of Christ chose to meet together constantly, because meeting with each other was meeting with *Him*: the glorious, never-changing, lavish-in-

His-displays-of-love Bridegroom who could never fail to meet with them when they met with Him. Their consistency of gathering, first evidenced in that famous passage in Acts 2, did not become so regular because their rituals needed to become routine. They were simply overjoyed to be together and, thus, with Jesus. You couldn't have *stopped* their ecstatic excitement to come and be with Him.

Really, there's much more New Testament evidence for *daily* gathering than there is for *weekly*; yet what most mattered was the spirit and purpose for which they gathered. In Troas, we see the brothers and sisters together, yes, on a Sunday, but they just couldn't get enough of each other – *and* the teaching – and things kept going and going and going…

> *"On the first day of the week we came together to break bread. Paul spoke to the people and, because he intended to leave the next day, kept on talking until midnight. There were many lamps in the upstairs room where we were meeting." (Acts 20)*

How much more fun to need to light additional lamps to keep our experience of Jesus going, rather than keeping tabs on our hour-long progress through a tri-fold bulletin! How much more joy must Jesus feel when our delight is in being near to Him, regardless of time, regardless of schedule, regardless of *anything.*

Personally, one of my favorite passages of time to imagine in the history of the Early Church occurred when Paul stayed put in Ephesus for an extended period. Here it is:

> *"He took the disciples with him and had discussions daily in the lecture hall of Tyrannus. This went on for two years, so that all the Jews and Greeks who lived in the province of Asia heard the word of the Lord." (Acts 19)*

Can you imagine all the lively, hilarious, rich, intense, beautiful, wondrous glories of Jesus they discovered together in *two whole years* of such "discussions"? One wonders how much of Paul's personal revelation of Jesus was unearthed in that constant, ongoing experience of being together in His presence – everyday. How those two years probably flew by for all of them! That's the sort of constant joyous atmosphere we're after!

CONCLUSION: We cannot authentically emulate the experiences of the Early Church gatherings without a constant coming-together, *both weekly and daily*. Our weekly time will be a larger-group gathering – which is being formed by this document – but the daily expression is a subject for our mutual discussion and decision...

How do you personally think the day-by-day nature of the Early Church gatherings can best be recaptured in our modern lives today? Let's be especially attentive to listen on this question. To me, it matters so deeply.

YOUR CONCLUSIONS:

X.

DEVOID OF SELF & DESIROUS TO SERVE

Have you ever wondered why, apart from the Apostles and the few others that Paul and John and Acts specifically mention, we don't know more of the individuals' names who made up the Early Church gatherings? You might think, given the importance of all they were doing for the sake of the Gospel, for Jesus Himself, that we'd be well-served to know more of their individual heroic stories.

They would heartily disagree. You see, within the colors and strands – the warp and the weft – of the tapestry of the Kingdom of Heaven, these people delighted to lay down their lives, their pride, their "Self," so that the Pattern – the Image of Jesus – was the only thing visible. They chose to die to self so that their Savior would always live. They replaced the nonsense defenses of their *id* and *ego* with the offensive strategies of service seen in the life and ministry of Jesus. You and I are reading – and writing – these words because they chose that lifestyle.

Listen to the sort of spirit that Paul suggested to the Roman gathering:

> *"Be devoted to one another in love. Honor one another above yourselves... Share with the Lord's people who are in need. Practice hospitality... Rejoice with those who rejoice; mourn with those who mourn. Live in harmony with one another. Do not be proud, but be willing to associate with people of low position." (Romans 12)*

As it pertains to how you live your life in the presence of other people – *especially* within the gathering – here's the advice that Paul is giving you:

1. Be devoted to the other person *(not yourself)* in love

2. Honor the other person, *not yourself*

3. Share your things with the other person *(not just yourself)*

4. Elevate the comfort and enjoyment of the other person *(not just your own)*

5. Where the other person *(not yourself)* is rejoicing, rejoice with the other person *(regardless of yourself)*

6. Where the other person *(not yourself)* is mourning, mourn with the other person *(regardless of yourself)*

7. Live your whole life so that it creates harmony with the other person *(not being so concerned for your own personal tranquility)*

8. Think not first of *yourself (your accomplishments, your personal grandeur, your sheer quality)* but associate willingly with the other person, regardless of their worldly stature.

In essence, given the choice between oneself and the other person, Paul is looking us in the eye and recommending – both *in* and *by* the spirit of Jesus – to *choose the other person*. Oh, what freedom we'd feel if we'd fully enjoy this Christ-attribute! It's what our gathering, and its leaders, must always be pursuing together.

Yet consider one of the main earthly/worldly/fleshly stumbling-blocks that will immediately come against this sort of others-first attitude:

> *"My brothers and sisters, believers in our glorious Lord Jesus Christ must not show favoritism. Suppose a man comes into your meeting wearing a gold ring and fine clothes, and a poor man in filthy old clothes also comes in. If you show special attention to the man wearing fine clothes and say, 'Here's a*

good seat for you,' but say to the poor man, 'You stand there' or 'Sit on the floor by my feet,' have you not discriminated among yourselves and become judges with evil thoughts? Listen, my dear brothers and sisters: Has not God chosen those who are poor in the eyes of the world to be rich in faith and to inherit the kingdom he promised those who love him? But you have dishonored the poor. Is it not the rich who are exploiting you? Are they not the ones who are dragging you into court? Are they not the ones who are blaspheming the noble name of him to whom you belong? If you really keep the royal law found in Scripture, 'Love your neighbor as yourself,' you are doing right. But if you show favoritism, you sin and are convicted by the law as lawbreakers." (James 2)

In the Roman world of yesterday and in the western world we inhabit today, perceived differences of "class" can lead so quickly to diminishment of a person's inherent value. Without a conscious thought, we "size each other up" to assign position; we are steeped in such stratification from our youth – no matter how we grew up.

How important, then, that we *throw off* such considerations within the gathering; that we model the earnest equalizing gaze with which Jesus looked into every face. Even our leaders may be of totally different social class (speaking in the world's economy) but none of that must matter in terms of how we welcome each other, love each other, delight in each other. Just see how readily the gathering in Sidon was prepared to welcome and care for their unexpected wandering friend, the Apostle Paul:

"The next day we landed at Sidon; and Julius, in kindness to Paul, allowed him to go to his friends so they might provide for his needs." (Acts 27)

We too must be so promptly prepared to provide for the practical needs of our people; imagine how the centurion, Julius, witnessed the Gospel because of the Sidonian's hospitality. Everything he'd probably already heard from Paul now rang true. So let's look at how the Early Church pooled their resources to account for such needs:

> *"Now about the collection for the Lord's people: Do what I told the Galatian churches to do. On the first day of every week, each one of you should set aside a sum of money in keeping with your income, saving it up, so that when I come no collections will have to be made. Then, when I arrive, I will give letters of introduction to the men you approve and send them with your gift to Jerusalem." (1 Corinthians 16)*

As our gathering isn't meant to supplant people's attendance and giving in their present church, we won't be planning on an "offering plate" to be a normal part of our time together. However, it *might* be fun to have a "free-will offering" dropbox inside the entry, where we could ongoingly collect money for a monthly "democratic disbursement," ie. at the end of each month, announcing the total collected, we could then offer the gathering a vote on where we give it away; specific people or projects or missions could be offered up on a rotating basis.

Finally, as discussed in Chapters VI & VIII, there may come times when people within the gathering find themselves at odds – whether personally, in business, or on a specific spiritual matter. If so, I cannot overstate how important is the following text for our consideration; may we learn to mirror the complete selflessness that Paul suggests:

> *"If any of you has a dispute with another, do you dare to take it before the ungodly for judgment instead of before the Lord's people? Or do you not know that the Lord's people will judge the world? And if you are to judge the world, are you not competent to judge trivial cases? Do you not know that we will judge angels? How much more the things of this life! Therefore, if you have disputes about such matters, do you ask for a ruling*

THE LANTERN OUT OF DOORS

from those whose way of life is scorned in the church? I say this to shame you. Is it possible that there is nobody among you wise enough to judge a dispute between believers? But instead, one brother takes another to court — and this in front of unbelievers! The very fact that you have lawsuits among you means you have been completely defeated already. Why not rather be wronged? Why not rather be cheated?" (1 Corinthians 6)

May our gathering be marked by *such* a mutual striving after selflessness that we'd each race to be the party who is *most* wronged, cheated, slighted. Let us learn together the heart that Jesus wants: the heart that leads the "other cheek" to turn and take the second blow for Him. And if we find that there are disagreements among us that need a council of brothers and sisters for resolution, let us selflessly offer ourselves to serve in that capacity. But may we *never* be defined to outsiders by dissent and dispute! Certainly, among us "there is *somebody* wise enough to judge a dispute between believers!"

In all of this, our only model, our only hope, our only source of strength, as always, will be Jesus Himself:

"This is how we know what love is: Jesus Christ laid down his life for us. And we ought to lay down our lives for our brothers and sisters. If anyone has material possessions and sees a brother or sister in need but has no pity on them, how can the love of God be in that person? Dear children, let us not love with words or speech but with actions and in truth." (1 John 3)

CONCLUSION: The Early Church gatherings, though comprised of various, very different individuals, were imbued with power because of the selfless servanteartedness of each of those various, very different individuals. Together, they sought to care for "the other person," not just for themselves, and they worked to rid their hearts of the worldly ways of

assigning value to people. They constantly served each other and their neighbors wholeheartedly, with love. They were generous, kind, and willing to be wronged for the sake of Jesus. This sort of spirit must always animate our hearts; we must, day by day, lay down our lives within the pattern of Jesus Himself.

YOUR CONCLUSIONS:

THE LANTERN OUT OF DOORS

XI.

PARTAKERS TOGETHER OF THE BREAD & THE WINE

Imagine if you yourself were a new believer who worshipped in one of the Early Church gatherings and you'd just caught wind of an upcoming visit from one of "the originals." Peter or John or Nathanael or Matthew – it doesn't really matter which – one of them was soon to be arriving to pay your fellowship a personal visit. How excited you would've been to meet this man; how many questions would've crowded your mind to ask him immediately upon his arrival. This was a person who had *personally* walked three years of days with the One who'd already entered your own heart and changed absolutely everything.

Amidst the excitement of the Apostle's arrival, his presence, his teaching, his personal witness to the life and Way of Jesus, I'd have to imagine something else that might've caught your attention: the way, upon preparing to receive the bread and wine – the Body and Blood – his whole countenance changed; the way he prepared his mind and spirit to receive, once again, His Lord.

THAT is the way we must receive the elements together. And, yes, we *must* be fellow-partakers of the bread and wine. One of the most important reasons we must do so is given quite bluntly by Paul in the chapter that precedes his communion teachings in 1 Corinthians:

> *"Is not the cup of thanksgiving for which we give thanks a participation in the blood of Christ? And is not the bread that we break a participation in the body of Christ? Because there is one loaf, we, who are many, are one body, for we all share the one loaf." (1 Corinthians 10)*

When you and I share the bread and wine together, we're

not only "participating" in the body and blood of Jesus, we are forever proclaiming our "one body" unity. For communion literally means "union together" – with Him *and* each other. It is a spiritual experience of His death and life within us.

So let's consider, then, Paul's well-known words on how we partake of it – this is all we need to know to shape our gathering's experience of communion:

> *"For I received from the Lord what I also passed on to you: The Lord Jesus, on the night he was betrayed, took bread, and when he had given thanks, he broke it and said, 'This is my body, which is for you; do this in remembrance of me.' In the same way, after supper he took the cup, saying, 'This cup is the new covenant in my blood; do this, whenever you drink it, in remembrance of me.' For whenever you eat this bread and drink this cup, you proclaim the Lord's death until he comes. So then, whoever eats the bread or drinks the cup of the Lord in an unworthy manner will be guilty of sinning against the body and blood of the Lord. Everyone ought to examine themselves before they eat of the bread and drink from the cup. For those who eat and drink without discerning the body of Christ eat and drink judgment on themselves." (1 Corinthians 11)*

Without all sorts of pre-ceremony, let us simply remind each other of the importance of our confession and preparation, and then, together, take the bread and wine – His Body and Blood. May we ever be mindful of the seriousness with which Jesus spoke of this eventual meal when He said to His disciples: "Most certainly I tell you, unless you eat the flesh of the Son of Man and drink his blood, you don't have life in yourselves. He who eats my flesh and drinks my blood has eternal life, and I will raise him up at the last day. For my flesh is food indeed, and my blood is drink indeed. He who eats my flesh and drinks my blood lives in me, and I in him." (John 6)

CONCLUSION: Since "we, who are many, are one body," it's imperative that "we all share the one loaf" of His body and the one cup of His blood within our gathering. Directly before, we should have a time of quiet confession and preparation and then, together, enjoy the elements as Paul described the original occurrence. "His flesh is food indeed, and His blood is drink indeed." Together, "we who eat His flesh and drink His blood live in Him, and He in us."

YOUR CONCLUSIONS:

XII

WORSHIPPERS

Last but certainly not least, the Early Church gatherings were places where the worship of Jesus practically never ceased – whether in song or word or heart or deed. An outside visitor probably would've been looking around the room, trying to catch a glimpse of Jesus Himself, so *presently* did those people talk and sing and speak of Him. Isn't that what we want for our fellowship? That Jesus, should He choose to walk in incognito, would be personally blessed, personally addressed, by the spirit and structure of everything we do?

That's certainly the sense of Paul's admonitions to the Ephesian gathering:

> *"Be filled with the Spirit, speaking to one another with psalms, hymns, and songs from the Spirit. Sing and make music from your heart to the Lord, always giving thanks to God the Father for everything, in the name of our Lord Jesus Christ."* *(Ephesians 5)*

It's in the process of our "giving thanks to God the Father for everything in the name of our Lord Jesus," *while* "singing and making music from our hearts to the Lord" *by* "speaking to one another with psalms, hymns, and songs from the Spirit" ***that*** we will "be filled with the Spirit." Many congregants in many churches seem to think that they should *only* worship with abandon *after* they "feel" like they're "filled with the Spirit" – and not a moment before.

Not so.

You and I are called to be people whose *whole lives* are one continuous stream of worship, whether that's in speech or song or music or dance or, even, work. Our spiritual act of worship should always be *leading* our life and mood and intellect; never – and I truly mean, never – is it supposed to be the other way around. Let us learn to come together and raise our voices, raise our hands, raise our hearts, raise our spirits, to worship together in the very Throneroom of Heaven. Jesus' blood has already ensured that that's our worshipping reality. Now it's up to us to actively *engage* with that worshipping reality.

Practically speaking, it's important that we blend all types of worship-in-song to invite and include *all generations of worshippers* – both those who love hymns and those who enjoy more modern styles. However, individual "tastes" in worship will not be our foremost concern. Worshipping Jesus is our foremost and, really, only concern.

CONCLUSION: Everything in our gathering must be about worshipping Jesus. Everything we plan must gear the heart to worship Him. May our every consideration, our every hope, our every direct decision be made with *this* as our question: Does it lead to worship of Jesus?

YOUR CONCLUSIONS:

All Conclusions Compiled

I. Complete Belief in the Power of Prayer

The *spirit* of the gathering's prayer-life matters more than its *structure*. In the Early Church, they prayed constantly, intimately, fearlessly, emboldeningly, in unity, and – together – "for all people."

It would seem best that we should start our times together in open-ended, unguided prayer that is a reflection of our individual, and yet corporate, face-to-face intimacy with Jesus. Really, prayer should be the greatest characterization of our gathering.

II. Together in the Teachings of Jesus

The target of our teaching must be Jesus Himself – His incarnation, life, teachings, miracles, death, resurrection, ascension, and the inheritance He's given us. Our teachers must always approach *Him* before approaching the gathering. Their teaching must exhibit a flavor of that first-hand, original, "oral tradition" style that we see utilized by the original Disciples and Apostles. And that style can only be learned in the presence of Jesus Himself, by having personal experiences of His voice, His power, His present "aliveness."

Lastly, it would seem that teaching was neither less nor more important than any other element of the Early Church gatherings; that it was integral, but not the lofty thing we often make it. It was simply *part* of what happened whenever they came together. And so it must be for us, as well.

III. Complete Belief that Jesus and the Holy Spirit would Act, Speak and Lead by Direct Revelation

Our gathering should expect to see nothing less than everything we see Jesus and the Holy Spirit doing across the pages of the New Testament. But seeing is not believing. *Believing* is seeing. When it comes to our own decision-making and direct strategic initiatives, we must wait for, watch for, and be expectant of the evidence of His voice and action. We must be open to supernatural visions, physical manifestations, "signs and wonders"; we must be ready to heal and to see His Holy Spirit act through us.

And, again, it's the degree to which we'll *believe* wherein we'll see His ability to act, not the other way around. As Peter described the interconnection: "in the meantime you are guarded by the power of God operating *through your faith*" (1 Peter 1). Our collective, individual belief is the channel chosen by Jesus for the flowing of the power of the Kingdom of Heaven into the world around us. And oh! how He *longs* to pipeline that power into our midst!

IV. Attractive & Accepting, Exhibiting a "Kindness that Leads to Repentance"

It's the presence of Jesus, the power of His love, the perfection of His character, that attracts outsiders, creates desire, and convicts the human heart of sin. No churchly contrivance can ever match His hand upon a life. Nothing we can ever do can merit mention alongside *His* Way.

The Early Church gatherings didn't grow because the "teaching there was so good," the children's programs were the best, the worship was stylish, or because the building they met in was modern, inviting. The Early Church gatherings attracted people because *He* was there. Even people like Saul – a murderous, unhinged, hateful sort of villain – were included and invited and accepted into the midst of the gathering. It was the job of the Holy Spirit to convict such people of sin. It was the gathering's job to "lift up" Jesus alone.

V. Practical

Our gathering must readily embrace the practicality and the smart, simple practices of the Early Church gatherings. From our discussion of that passage in Acts 2, to our format according to the sharing of tongues and prophets, to the location and consistency and duration of our times, to the sense of "home" we desire to create – all of it must lend itself to the peace of God and the creation of a gathering that points to Jesus alone. The exact details may shift and change over time, but not the non-negotiability of His presence being our highest goal together.

VI. Indivisible & Focused on Unity – Open to All the Gifts

Jesus has specifically chosen individuals like us to be spiritually united by Him into a cohesive unit that actually *is* Him – His "Body." This Body attains its unity only by keeping its eyes on Him, operating from the giftings of His Holy Spirit, and by settling for nothing less than a complete oneness. When issues arise between us, constructive steps must immediately be taken, and yet the focus on unity can never flag: a Body cannot be split and live. We must accept and live from the fullness of our calling *together*. We must pursue Him *together* or we can't attain to His fullness.

VII. Led by Shepherds who Bear the Stamp of Jesus

Leadership in the Early Church gatherings was a calling directly from Jesus; the leaders were viewed as shepherds called by *the* Good Shepherd. We must look for the same call and the same heart in our leaders. They must be people who *currently* answer to the descriptions offered up in Paul's instructions to Timothy; leadership in the gathering is not the staging ground to *learn* leadership. We're looking for people whose natural intimacy with Jesus creates a teachable, teaching spirit that attracts all people they meet to Him alone.

VIII. Encouraged by, and Encouraging with, the Spirit of Jesus

The Early Church gatherings were a people encouraged by, and encouraging others with, the direct encouraging spirit of Jesus. They always lived by His encouragement and were led by people who encouraged them deeply, just as He Himself had encouraged His own disciples.

Let us always consider – *before* and *after* any time we gather – whether that encouraging/encouraged spirit has both welcomed-in and also sent out our brothers and sisters. Heavy-heartedness was not in evidence in the Early Church. And it should never be a fruit of our present gatherings in His Name.

IX. They Gathered Together Constantly

We cannot authentically emulate the experiences of the Early Church gatherings without a constant coming-together, *both weekly and daily*. Our weekly time will be a larger-group gathering – which is being formed by this document – but the daily expression is a subject for our mutual discussion and decision…

X. Devoid of Self & Desirous to Serve

The Early Church gatherings, though comprised of

various, very different individuals, were imbued with power because of the selfless servantheartedness of each of those various, very different individuals. Together, they sought to care for "the other person," not just for themselves, and they worked to rid their hearts of the worldly ways of assigning value to people. They constantly served each other and their neighbors wholeheartedly, with love. They were generous, kind, and willing to be wronged for the sake of Jesus. This sort of spirit must always animate our hearts; we must, day by day, lay down our lives within the pattern of Jesus Himself.

XI. Partakers Together of the Bread & the Wine

Since "we, who are many, are one body," it's imperative that "we all share the one loaf" of His body and the one cup of His blood within our gathering. Directly before, we should have a time of quiet confession and preparation and then, together, enjoy the elements as Paul described the original occurrence. "His flesh is food indeed, and His blood is drink indeed." Together, "we who eat His flesh and drink His blood live in Him, and He in us."

XII. Worshippers

Everything in our gathering must be about worshipping Jesus. Everything we plan must gear the human heart to worship Him. May our every consideration, our every hope, our every direct decision be made with *this* as our question: Does it lead to worship of Jesus?

PREPARATIONS AND QUESTIONS TO BE ANSWERED[3]

Prior to a first gathering –

1. Consider this document, and your combined conclusions throughout, with the planning group. Discuss. Make decisions. Pray.

2. Decide on a location.

3. From within the initial planning group, consider the giftings and callings of each person. Decide specifically where and how each is called to serve. Make sure that the *Apostle, Prophet, Evangelist, Pastor* and *Teacher* roles are all represented within this initial group of leaders.

4. Set a date to start. Begin to invite people desirous of the "more" that Jesus always offers.

5. Pray without ceasing.

Questions to be answered –

1. Where will we gather?

2. What role will "the breaking of bread" play, ie. Will we have a meal together ever week? Once a month? How will we facilitate the food and serving?

3. How can we offer the chance to give

---

[3] These preparations and questions are being written prior to our planning group's first meeting. Therefore, many gaps and questions for consideration will also be filled in later. If you're not part of the Colorado Springs gathering, feel free to contact Eugene with questions and preparation-steps of your own.

contributions toward our "democratic disbursement," as described in Chapter X?

4. Are there other ways we can practically connect people in need with people willing to give to those specific needs?

5. How can we best integrate different styles of music for our times of worship?

6. How should we facilitate the "tongues and prophets" sharing time? Should there be a small group that hears people's offerings and then gets them "booked" for future weeks?

7. Regarding prayer and healing, should we have teams of people – gifted in each – who are perpetually available throughout each gathering for anyone to approach?

RECOMMENDED FORMAT
A Best Guess, Based on The Early Church Gatherings

Meal together[4]

1. Open, and open-ended, time of prayer

2. Welcome, Announcements[5], Reminder of availability of prayer & healing teams throughout

3. Time of worship in song

4. Open-format sharing (tongues, prophets, testimonies, as prepared in coordination with our team)

5. Time of response from gathering

6. Time of worship in song

7. Teaching of Jesus

8. Time of response from gathering

9. Time of worship in song

10. Sharing the Bread & Wine

11. Any final words or exhortations from within the gathering?

12. Prayer of alignment

---

[4] Again, our planning team needs to decide how/when we will facilitate "breaking bread" together.

[5] Including, monthly, a "vote" on where to give away accumulated funds

ABOUT THE AUTHOR

Eugene lives in Colorado with his wife, Jenny, and their children – Hadley, Tripp and Hoyt. He is the director of The Union, a project of The New Horizons Foundation.

If you'd like to talk, or even meet in person, feel free to contact him by email at eugeneluning@gmail.com

Made in the USA
San Bernardino, CA
15 July 2016